Story Seeds for Fantastical Trees - A Collection of Writing Prompts 1

Writing Prompts, Volume 1

Mara Lynn Johnstone

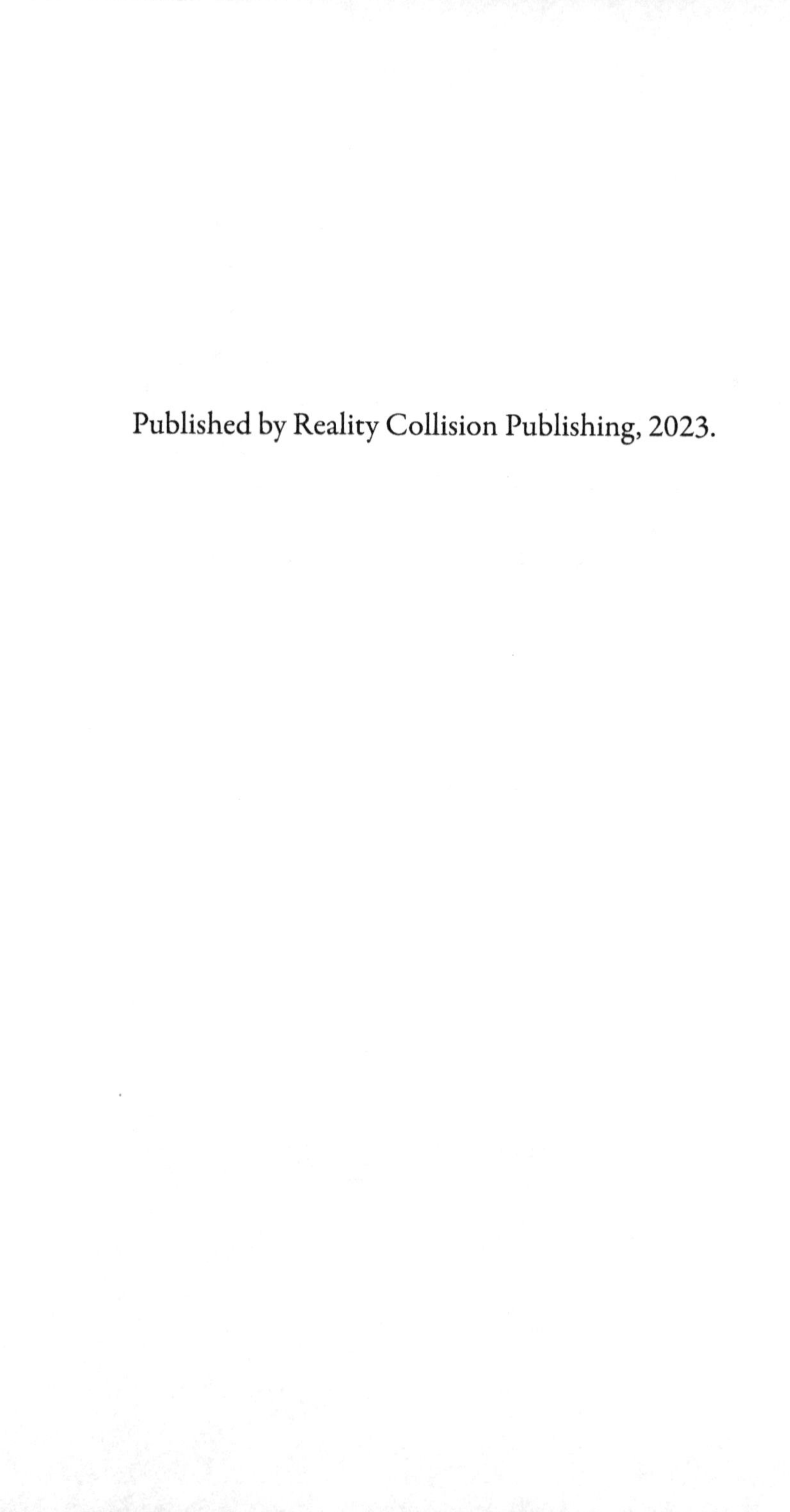

Published by Reality Collision Publishing, 2023.

STORY SEEDS FOR FANTASTICAL TREES - A COLLECTION OF WRITING PROMPTS 1

First edition. May 29, 2023.

Copyright © 2023 Mara Lynn Johnstone.

ISBN: 979-8223451877

Written by Mara Lynn Johnstone.

Also by Mara Lynn Johnstone

Writing Prompts
Story Seeds for Fantastical Trees - A Collection of Writing Prompts 1

Standalone
Spectacular Silver Earthling
A Swift Kick to the Thorax

Watch for more at https://www.MaraLynnJohnstone.com.

1

Tell me about fantasyland pirates. With peg legs made of enchanted wood, which can be planted over the buried treasure to grow into a magnificent treehouse. Or planted on the seashore, to grow into a new ship.

Pirates with an eyepatch covering the eye that can see into your soul, because that sort of thing is distracting in everyday life.

Pirates with intelligent parrots — a bird that is a crewmate in its own right, while the two-legger walking around is the decoy golem. Or a bird that is actually a dragon, temporarily in bird form, just waiting for the chance to show the enemy ships why they should be feared.

Pirates who have never owned a boat, though they've sunk a great many, because what use would merfolk have for a boat?

Tell me about fantasyland pirates.

2

Which do you think would be more powerful: that which was once alive, or that which has been infused with life? It's two very different approaches to magic.

Formerly alive: magic spun from hair, ground up fingernails, teardrops, blood. These are things that were once part of a living being, and some life still clings to them.

Infused with life: beloved teddy bears. Dolls handed down through the generations. The favorite pen, which has had its ink replaced many times over the years, and has filled so many notebooks that it feels like a treasured friend. A painting of a loved one. The family car.

I can't tell you which type would win every time, but I can say it would make for a fascinating showdown. And I've love to see a blood mage get creamed by Mom's station wagon. *It's been a part of this family for thirty years, and it will not stand for that.*

3

When I first heard about "companion ponies," I thought the idea was fascinating and perfect for a fantasy setting. Specifically in the field of competitive dragonriding. As it turns out, racehorses in our world are regularly assigned ponies as best friends, to keep them company and offer emotional stability. Horse racing is stressful, after all, and horses are herd animals. Having even just one herdmate can make an enormous difference to their mental health (and thus their performance).

That's our world. What kind of animal would be assigned to racing dragons? Smaller, flightless dragons? Cats? Capybaras?

I wonder if the companion animal could even pull double duty in protecting against sabateurs. A dragon whose friend was stolen away would be distressed, and not at the top of their game. Maybe the campanion animals can fend for themselves. Llama. Firebird. Pitbull. Goose. Firebird goose that sleeps lightly and can honk loud enough to damage a human's hearing. The possibilities are endless!

4

Picture the early days when teleporters weren't quite safe. A person could lose an arm by appearing too close to a wall — molecules occupying the same space would cause an antimatter reaction and blip out of existence. You might write something about this time period.

Or perhaps about the time shortly after, when "shoving protocols" were implemented, making sure that any pre-existing walls were politely pushed aside.

There's also another possibility, on the less ethical side of things. Maybe it's a time of war. Maybe money or a grudge is involved. Maybe we'll never know why, but someone realizes that they can weaponize the old version of the teleportation tech.

Throw some random junk in your teleporter, and use it to blow a hole in an enemy spaceship's hull. Or a bank vault. Or an oncoming asteroid. And of course this is a great way of getting rid of dangers, like a bomb or a toxic substance. Or evidence of a crime. Or witnesses. Or, depending on who's doing the inventing, the villains. (Who would even think of threatening an innocent with that; how dare you *sir?*)

5

Write a fairytale in reverse. Pick a classic story, jot down the bare bones of the plot, then figure out how to build a different story around them in that order.

The Little Mermaid: a human who's unable to speak trades her life on land for one in the sea where she can sing like anything.

Red Riding Hood: a girl from town and a man from the woods bring a wolf back to life. The wolf responds by attacking the girl's grandmother. Whether she survives, or, perhaps, poisons him with food brought by the girl, is up to you.

Sleeping Beauty: a princess's first kiss causes her to fall into enchanted sleep for a long time, during which the dense forests in the land all die off. When she wakes, her suitor is gone, and she has to contend with the magic-wielding rival responsible for the curse.

There are a lot of possibilities here.

6

The idea of alien aesthetics has always been one that's under-explored in movies. The audience needs to know right away if these are the good guys! The ships should look sleek and futuristic! Never mind the fact that cultures on Earth have wildly different ideas about what looks good, never mind what actual aliens might think.

Even just color schemes could be unexpected: alien warriors who consider pink and pastel to be the most intimidating, or diplomats who project a calm dignity in their neon camo patterns.

Spaceships could be shaped like anything. Maybe an alien culture thinks it's good luck for their vessels to resemble food items, to invite fortune and keep their food from spoiling on long voyages. Humans would find this funny. Humans would have to work to keep from laughing when presented with a shiny new warship built in their honor — the UES Slice Of Pizza. Some humans would hate this intensely, while others consider it the best thing ever.

What if the Earth had rings like Saturn? They would be spectacular, especially when lit by the sun. The view would be different depending on what part of the planet you were on.

How would this shape the various creation myths and cosmologies? Surely there would be multiple explanations for where those shapes in the sky came from.

What would it be like for the first person from the equator to venture far from home? What kind of stories can you tell about it?

8

I recently saw an art prompt for a vampire centaur, and that brings up a whole range of possibilities. Combine your cryptids! Either fantasy land species, or paranormal entities.

Goblin werewolf.

Alien abductions done by dragons. (Maybe they use holograms of humanoid shapes, but can't bring themselves to include hair or non-draconian flesh tones, thus the "little green men.")

Maybe the scientist who turned himself invisible was part fae and didn't know it, and that's why his science went wrong.

Lots of possibilities here!

Here's a fictional interaction that I'd like to see: four characters who are partly robotic and partly meat creatures, discussing their relationships with humanity.

Cyborg A (born human, was injured): "I grapple with my lost humanity."

Cyborg B (born human, chose this): "Humanity was holding me back."

Construct A (only looks human): "I want what you two had."

Construct B (built for a specific function): "What are you on about? Humans are disgusting. Leave me out of this."

10

When I was a kid, first hearing about "black light," I expected a reverse lightbulb that sucked all the light from the room, casting solid shadows on everything in its path. It could be useful, I reasoned, for summer bedtimes when the sky was too bright to sleep. Or for people who worked night jobs and slept during the day. Or for burglars, keeping themselves anonymous in a permanent patch of shadow. There could be many uses, I was sure; the grownups must have come up with something very clever indeed.

They didn't. Write about someone who did.

11

For someone living their whole life in space, never going planetside, the entire concept of dirt would be unimaginably gross. We don't even think about it other than a quick washing of hands here and there, but just picture it from a foreign perspective.

Dirt is a mix of rock dust, dried plant bits, rotten plant bits, dead animal bits, fungus, and poop.

If someone from a space station encounters that for the first time, they're going to be torn between reaching for the hand sanitizer or the religious symbols first.

12

Take a cliche that you hate and turn it around. Reverse it completely, or change the genders, or tweak details and add things until it becomes worth using in a story.

Personally, I hate the movie trope of the clueless guy who gets trained by an old master as The One Best Hope ... when the love interest is right there, an established student of the old master, or otherwise already an expert. I hate that a lot. So I might write a story where there is no inept male hero, or where the clueless guy convinces the master that the female expert is a much better choice of hero. Or maybe things go according to Hollywood standard, until it bothers the girl so much that she leaves to join the bad guys.

What cliches or tropes bother you? Convenient comas, evil twins, kids' stories where the parents are inexplicably oblivious to all the magic and adventure going on? See what you can do to change it up until it's *better*.

13

Mad scientists are fun, but I think there's a lot more untapped potential in mad wizards. The kind of magic-user to ask questions that didn't occur to other people, and to actually test them out, for better or worse (usually worse).

Regular wizards ask questions like "If dragon scales are fireproof, can I grind one up and mix it with wood pulp to get fireproof paper?"

Mad wizards wonder "Since touching pixie dust makes people fly, what would happen if I ate some? Can I build up an internalized flight reservoir, or will I just get an upset digestive track, and have to clean it off the bathroom ceiling?"

14

What are some unexplored uses for an echolocation-style sense of one's surroundings? If you can tell with a mental blink exactly where everything is, then you'll have a leg up on anyone who gets by with only eyesight.

You could put that ability to use in childcare, finding lost toys and hidden children, as well as dangers.

You would be welcome in search and rescue: faster than the dogs in locating unconscious people among rubble.

You'd make a talented lockpick, cutpurse, or burglar if your morality leans in that direction. A VIP on any heist.

You'd be in high demand for clearing minefields, digging for gold, locating termite infestations, and finding all of the sewing needles that your neighbor's cat just knocked into the shag carpet. Again.

15

What if vampirism was transmitted by mosquito?

My high school science teacher told us of a hiking trip he was on, when his friends started making fun of him for all the bug spray he was putting on.

His reply was "I have dormant malaria in my bloodstream. I want to make sure that anything that bites me is dead before it gets to you."

After that, they kept spraying him with more whenever his back was turned.

That sounds like an ideal scenario for half-vampires, or "dormant" vampirism.

16

What would be the best choice of housepet for the various supernatural/fantasy types?

I could see a cat getting along well with a dragon. Centaurs might be spooked by dogs, though werewolves may consider them just part of the pack.

Maybe unicorns would enjoy helper monkeys, with those little fingers that are oh so useful for the things that magic can't do.

Obvious choices for a vampire would be bats, rats, or maybe cats, though if you want something truly long-lived, it's hard to beat a tortoise. And what about parrots? Relatively long-lived, intelligent, and trainable for saying ominous things when humans wander in. Some even come in properly gothic grays.

17

Why do clones always come out of the cloning vat with the same hairstyle as the original? Better options:

* No hair at all

* Hair the same length as the original, but unstyled

* Hair that has been left to grow wild and free for all the apparent years that the person has been alive. Body hair and beard too where applicable. With lots of joke potential about "Clone Van Winkle" and "Bropunzel."

18

What if the rules about what a necromancer could control were oddly loose? Say they could manipulate anything that was once "dead" – by a very strict definition that involves the lack of a pulse.

That adds to the list of controllable things: corpses, zombies, ghosts, vampires ... and that guy whose heart stopped that one time.

Oh, and those frogs that hibernate by freezing solid. Them too.

"Go, my minions! Thaddeus, you bite them; Bob, stop complaining and throw a torch or something; and WartyFace ... you get to sneak up behind them and croak really loud. Go!"

19

Write about a Magical Companion Animal that's much bigger than the human.

Maybe a witch turns down cats in favor of an elephant who can help with the magic spells. That trunk can hold things, after all. And there's amusing potential for Dumbo-style flying.

Or maybe the Prophesied Peasant of Destiny meets something in the woods to help them on their journey — a moose instead of a unicorn. Woe betide anyone who gets on their bad side.

This can be sci-fi too, since everybody loves a spaceship mascot. Instead of a shoulder-riding pet, this ship has a furry blob that likes being a beanbag chair for the crew. It's handy if space pirates attack — it can plug a hole in the hull, and give any boarders an inescapable bear hug.

20

I'd love to see more urban werewolves. Even the most well-adjusted of lycanthropes seem to crave running through the forest like nothing else, maybe chasing down a prey animal or two. What other outlet is there for that?

Urban werewolf jogging clubs, treadmill champions, parkour teams. Flag football. Sprawling city-wide scavenger hunts on a timer, with the winner to decide where they get dinner, and the loser buying.

Heck, they don't even have to go on foot. Werewolf motorcycle gangs, car races, skateboard parks! Werewolf roller derbies! The sky's the limit.

21

Consider fantasyland creatures with camouflage and mimicry.

Rock trolls look like boulders, yes. But what about the predatory hobgoblins that look like sheep, and can lead away part of the herd?

Gnomes that blend in with a patch of mushrooms if you don't look too closely.

Freshwater mermaids with pebbly skin and hair like algae.

Small dragons that flat-out shapeshift to look like housecats, because they want in on that good life. Mice to eat, a fire to sleep beside, and the freedom to steal coins from the couch cushions — that's a fine life right there. (And woe betide any burglar!)

22

Here's a superpowered idea for you: write about a superhero whose powers don't match their name and costume. Perhaps they dress like this on purpose, and they confuse the villains every time.

If a hero is decked out in flame patterns, after all, then the obvious way to defeat them is with a surprise garden hose. But if that water suddenly turns into ice knives that go flying back at the villain, there would be an understandable amount of panicking.

Especially if the next person to meet that hero finds them dressed in plant patterns, and misunderstands their powers all over again.

23

I've seen plenty of fantasy stories set in a vague medieval period, and modern ones as well, but precious few set in the spacefaring future. I'm talking about a world with all the standard fantasy races, just a few centuries farther along the timeline.

Just picture it:

Elvish spaceships are elegant things, environmentally friendly and sleek. Goblin ships lose pieces every time they launch, and if a ship lands with a full crew it's considered a wild success.

Dwarves are the masters of all things cybernetic and mecha. Their war machines are legendary, surpassed only by their construction mechs.

Unicorns are accompanied by helper robots for the mundanities that require hands. (Telekinesis and other magic use is so gauche in public.) The robots come in many types, from human-sized to spiderlike, all with many pockets. The most popular model is the monkey. No one is really sure why.

24

Among a list of nicknames for Hephaestus, the Greek god of blacksmithing, is "sooty god." This makes me think that there really ought to be a story where Cinderella gets a patron god. They'd get along so well.

Cinders; soot. Mistreated by stepfamily (made a servant in her own home); mistreated by Olympians (thrown off Olympus because he was born disabled).

Maybe she impresses the prince by crafting something more epic than a shoe. Maybe she just leaves and starts her own blacksmithing business, with no need for a man. Maybe she gets *vengeance*.

I'm just saying, there's potential.

25

What would happen if every human in the world was suddenly invulnerable, unable to be injured whatsoever? (You get to decide whether they can still die, age, or get sick.)

The hard-hat industry would go under. Extreme sports would explode. There might arise a whole new type of sport/ fight/demolition derby. Criminal sorts would have a grand time discovering how high they'd have to jump from in order to break through a bank ceiling. Though they would of course get a chance to stress-test the jail too, since just because you can't be hurt doesn't mean you can't be caught.

26

After seeing yet another piece of media where the bad guys lure out the good guys by being public bullies (because everyone knows that a hero will *always* break cover to rescue someone), I would like to see it go a different way.

I want to see a villain threaten an innocent, and instead of the expected hero bursting onto the scene, they get a different villain.

Because sometimes villainy is about being pure evil, and other times it's just about doing whatever you want, with no one to stop you.

And sometimes what you want is to obliterate the person being evil to an innocent.

27

Someday I'll figure out how mermaid society works without answering every question with magic. Do you think they light up their houses with bioluminescence, or have they evolved in dark water able to do everything blind? Maybe there are different cultures for freshwater and deep sea.

The cultures with glowing plankton in jars everywhere would look the most magical. And only in merfolk homes will you hear the phrase "Hang on; I gotta feed the lightbulb."

28

If a time traveler wanted to make an offshoot timeline that was as disrupted as possible in terms of evolution, what animal should they introduce to the dinosaur era?

Housecats are famous for wiping out small animals, but there were a lot of big ones around then. Perhaps a population of tigers?

Cockroaches are expected to take over the world after a nuclear misadventure. Would they get a solid foothold early on?

Rabbits breed quickly and eat many plants. Would the undergrowth of that time period be to their liking?

What about goats? Bears? Moose or buffalo, ready to fight? Or (perhaps this is cheating) humans?

And how would that species or its descendants cope with the impending comet?

29

What's the difference between a superhero in a fantasy setting and just a regular enchanted adventurer? Largely the theatrics.

Just picture it: a dragon is driven out of the hills by other monsters encroaching on the territory, and it starts harassing a human settlement. The townsfolk send word to the queen for someone to confront it. Instead of a knight in clanking armor on horseback, the requested hero arrives from the sky. Wearing brightly colored clothes and a cape.

Then they make friends with the dragon, and go off with it to punch the rock trolls who invaded its territory. Or not. The rest is up to you.

Put a cool skater-dude character into a fantasy setting, ready to do kickflips on a broom and call everything gnarly.

Is he an accidental transplant from our world, ready to roll with it (and make jokes about rolling on a skateboard)? I'll bet he'd love to learn broom riding.

Or is he from this world, just eccentric? Surely only the coolest magicians stand on brooms when they fly. Maybe he learned a few tricks and terminology from studying Earth, or maybe he's just that tubular on his own.

31

Your character can suddenly hear their own theme music, in the style of movies and video games. How do they use this power?

Do they know when it's safe to walk through dark neighborhoods?

Do they have a valuable insight on dating apps?

Do they take a moment to listen before making any major purchases? ("This used car sounds like the Benny Hill theme, so no. This one sounds like tragic opera music, so *definitely* no. This one's a romantic comedy. I can live with that.")

32

I love the idea of martial arts for nonhuman species. What would that *look* like, to face off with a centaur black belt? Lots of kicks, sure, but what kind of moves would they pull that the average human would be unprepared for?

They have body mass on their side, the better to knock a human off balance: just grab an arm and pull. They've got the height advantage, especially when they rear up: kick with a foreleg or slam a fist into the opponent on the way down. They wouldn't have to be as picky with their targets when kicking, since hooves hurt no matter where they land.

But horse legs are famously fragile. I'll bet they have to be much more careful to avoid injury when fighting. I can see leg armor being a thing. It would be an interesting tradeoff.

33

Urban fantasy cities with a wide range of species are interesting, because on the one hand, they're inconvenient and hard to plan for. (How do you build a public bathroom to accommodate everything from pixies to centaurs to intelligent slimes?)

But on the other hand, there are people for every niche, often suited to it more than humans would be.

Need an employee for the night shift? Sure! Plenty of nocturnal cryptids. Need somebody who can lift their bodyweight with a finger, or handle caustic chemicals, or climb to dangerous heights? Just check the box at the employment center; I'm sure somebody's ready and waiting.

Sometimes they might end up in the wrong job entirely, but that just makes things more interesting. ("I'm a fire elemental, not a water elemental! I can't clean up this spill! And no, a hazmat suit won't help!")

34

Here's a spooky sci-fi one for you: establish a character in a mech suit of some sort, whose face we never see. Then, in whichever way best fits the story, reveal that the character died long ago and the suit's AI has been impersonating them for reasons of its own.

This could be the story's villain of course, but it may be FAR more interesting if the AI is one of the good guys.

How is this revealed? Do the other characters find a record of the death? Is there a scan for life forms that clearly shows nothing in the suit? Does this turn out to be helpful, since the AI can effectively hide from the bad guys? What kind of story do you want to tell?

35

It's fun to overthink magic. If a character can control rain, what else does that mean they can do? Sure, you could go the cheap way out with a written spell for weather and nothing else, but there are many more intriguing options.

How does the character control rain, anyways? That could be pure telekinesis. If so, then they can likely control anything, or at least anything lightweight. Throw sand in someone's eyes, clean up spilled flour from baking, wipe car windshields of condensation/snow...

If the rain is controlled by water magic, then that's a different kettle of fish. Water is everywhere: blood, air, plants. A waterbender could control living things, not just rain.

If it's a general weather-based magic, either talking to the planet as a sentient being or simply causing things to change, then boy howdy there are some useful weather tricks out there. (Look up "heat burst" and tell me that wouldn't be handy to throw down on a villain.)

Honestly, it could be anything. The rules of magic are what you make them, and you can make them interesting indeed.

36

What's the strangest thing that an apocalypse could revolve around? Zombies are popular, followed by invading aliens, and an uprising of robots. But there are plenty of other supernatural creatures who might cause trouble, plus technological mishaps.

Sphinxes crawling out of the woodwork, demanding that world leaders answer riddles or be obliterated?

Unicorns charging at people, cattle, and cars? Winning every encounter?

Basilisks in the subway? Bigfoot eating the garden? Phoenixes sunning themselves on rooftops with an attitude of *Admire our glory; what do you mean this flat rock is flammable?*

What kind of apocalypse has never been done before?

37

Think back to the type of stories you liked as a young'un. What would Young You have wanted Grownup You to have written? Were there specific themes, aesthetics, characters you daydreamed about? Write something like that now. Change it as much as you like. Maybe the unicorns are predatory. Maybe the kid with super strength grows up to be an EMT instead of a superhero, and can rip open a crashed car all the faster. Maybe that species you made up that looks like a mess of animal parts thrown together turns out to be just that, thanks to genetic engineering or a young magician with far too much power at hand.

What would have Young You wanted to see, and how can you make it interesting to you now?

38

What are some uses for a magically animated tree? I'm thinking of the kind that moves, wrapping branches around things, throwing fruit if it feels so inclined. It could do a lot. For example:

Guards for the door/treasure/whatever. Ready to smack anyone without the password.

Guards for the children, playing in the yard. Holding up swings, lifting kids to where they can see the entire neighborhood, snaking a vine between two who are fighting, catching another when they trip. Raining hell and applesauce on anyone who tries to kidnap them.

Craftmaking assistant. So many branches, for holding paintings while they dry, sculptures while the glue sets, hand-dyed clothes out of reach of the cat. Working as extra hands for that complicated model ship assembly.

Animal exerciser! Throw a ball for the dog, dangle leaves for the cat. Get pooped on by the bird and not mind.

Really, a magical tree that's properly cared for can be incredibly useful. Just be sure that you treat it well. You don't want to be the one house on the street with the wilted tree. And you don't want to be the former owners of the house, who disappeared without a trace.

39

Time for a fantasyland heist!

What species and talents will you find among your trusty crew? Elves, goblins, intelligent owlbears? Shapeshifters and shadowmancers? Joe the plumber, who's mostly there as a distraction?

And now the big question: are they stealing from a dragon's hoard, a wizard's tower, or perhaps an unlikely combination of the two?

Maybe the dragon and the wizard are dating. Maybe one of them acquired a Thing, then they argued, and the other hid it. Then they made up and forgot. Now the heist team has to sneak in and find it without causing a ruckus.

Or, you know, it could be just about the money. But additional drama does make things more fun.

40

What if aliens landed, ready to meet dinosaurs instead of humans? Maybe the one in charge of navigation is new to this whole faster-than-light business, and didn't realize that the images they saw through telescopes were actually from millions of years ago. Maybe life on the aliens' planet evolved slowly, and they didn't expect anything to have changed. Or maybe they just didn't hear about the extinction event, and they assumed that they'd meet the descendants of velociraptors and troodons instead. (Uh, whoops? Greetings!)

41

Fire needs oxygen in order to burn.

Some planets don't have oxygen in their atmospheres.

Assuming life could evolve in such an environment, then there could conceivably be aliens out there who have never heard of the concept of fire.

Just imagine trying to explain it to them without sounding utterly delusional.

42

What kind of magic system would a child create? Depending on the age, I could see a style of "make it in Legos then a real one appears," or the classic "draw it then it leaps off the page," or maybe "video game controller also controls other things." Also, assuming there's a magical adult keeping an eye on things, what sort of parental controls might be added on to this power? Kids are infamous for big emotions and a lack of foresight, after all.

"Okay honey, the Xbox controller will only move things that weigh less than this teddy bear, and they won't move faster than this wind-up car. We don't want any windows broken."

43

People are always talking about worldbuilding limits to their magic, so here's one: magic wands with tiny power cartridges that need replacing.

Maybe the magic-user can make the cartridges, with some time and enchanting.

Maybe only certain people can do it, and will trade a specific list of things for them.

Maybe there's potential for a heist at the great mage-battery storage facility. (Who's in charge of the place, and how do they protect it? Is this fantasyland capitalism, or a dragon's hoard?)

44

I am entertained by the idea of a wizardly equivalent of a YouTube star. Somebody who tests new spells with a scrying mirror broadcasting it to all.

"This one's supposed to make a designated object levitate, but the last levitation spell I tried from this grimoire ended with an artistic spray of pixie dust and miscellaneous herbs across the ceiling — can you see that? Let me tilt the frame. Yeah, it's sparkly and pretty and no cleaning spell has been able to touch it. I've decided that it adds to the decor. Anyways, let's hope we don't get an uglier stripe today! I am wearing my oldest robe just in case."

45

Imagine jack-o-lanterns were a magical creature, maybe plants brought to life by an ill-advised magician. How would that work? Do some pumpkins start growing teeth, and you have to notice before they pop free of their stems to go bouncing around terrorizing the wildlife? Is there a population of wild ones roaming the woods, and you need to keep your garden well protected so they don't get in to bite your normal pumpkins? What happens if they bite a person?

Also worth considering is the fact that real jack-o-lanterns served as protection from various spooky things, warding them away from people's homes. Maybe, instead of being dangerous beasties, living ones would stand guard ready to face off against other dangerous things.

Or perhaps both. Guard dogs were bred from the same wolves they guard against, after all.

46

In the spacefuture when gravity is just something we can flip a switch for, imagine the possibilities for mundane little things.

Maybe it's common to keep one room or closet of your quarters at zero-g. You can keep delicate craft projects in there (glue this bit to the other bit without worrying that it'll collapse).

You can set up a tiny greenhouse for plants that grow nowhere else (360° flowers, perfectly spherical fruit, air roots going in all directions and leaves that tilt to follow the spaceship's lights).

Heck, you can read an obnoxiously heavy book in there without having to hold it up. And that's not even getting into the recreational uses for larger rooms. What else?

47

You know the trope of someone time-traveling from the past to the present day, and wacky hijinks ensue as they try to understand stuff? I'd love to see someone from the past be unexpectedly good at things.

Modern person: "Sorry, I don't have time to show you anything really interesting right now. I have to type up all these handwritten notes by tonight."

Monk from before the printing press: "You just press the letters, and they appear? CAN I HELP?"

48

Here's a sentence for you to interpret as you will:

"Life has been much easier since science invented magic."

What could this mean? What did science create? In my mind, magic is a way of affecting reality by means that shouldn't work, given our understanding of physics. Willpower, reciting an incantation, rubbing a lamp, waving a wand. How could scientists make that sort of thing exist?

And did they make all of it, or just one thing? Is the narrator exaggerating? Do they maybe not understand what happened? Did a scientist open a portal to fairyland, and reverse engineer some pixie dust?

How else could science invent magic?

49

Most fictional riding mounts are based on the most positive traits of horses — noble steeds, strong and fast, gentle giants, can travel long distances, etc. But what doesn't come up as much is the less glamorous details.

Thoroughbred horses are notorious for being flighty, getting startled by plastic bags and unfamiliar clothes, and any number of other things. What if a dragon did that?

And we all know how difficult it can be for a horse to fully heal a broken leg; plenty of cowboy stories feature shooting one's horse out of mercy. What if alien war steeds had a similarly fragile evolution? Winning a battle could be as simple as laying out unethical traps, either in stealth or in plain sight, to see if the enemy will take the risk.

Either that or litter the field with plastic bags and party balloons. Those war steeds would have no idea what they were up against.

50

Have you heard of albino plants? They can't make chlorophyll and are basically vampires, getting nutrients from the roots of other plants.

What if there were about albino dryads?

Would they go around biting other dryads? Stabbing their roots into things? Maybe they could adapt to drink blood. That would be the most terrifying vampire around. ("Wooden stake? that's cute.")

Or, on the other hand, they could be supported by their community like the regular albino plants are. Just picture all the other dryads twining their roots together to share energy.

Of course, both options are possible too.

51

Consider "weaponized allergies."

I'm picturing a wizard duel that ends when one wizard casts a spell that appears to do nothing, then the other starts coughing uncontrollably because of all the pollen in the meadow.

Or the space freighter with questionable morals who always manages to recover anything stolen by space pirates, since the cargo hold is booby-trapped with nanites that will make anyone allergic to trace elements found in the matter creators that make everyone's food this far out on the galactic rim.

I've heard of medications causing an allergy to alcohol, and *that* could definitely make for interesting scenarios.

Whether it's a medieval bard who's too fond of wine (and has a wizard friend ready to do something about it), or a space pirate whose love of Martian rum has made them one enemy too many (and this one is ready to sneak nanites into their food), I'll bet there's some drama about to go down.

52

Making up animals by combining real ones is always fun. My challenge for you now is to think up one that was created for a specific purpose — house pet, guard, livestock — then envision it in a very different scenario.

Mink + parrot = clever fursnake bred for the elites ... and an utter pest at the resort island when they escape and overpopulate.

Pit bull + crocodile = junkyard guardian ... and the caretaker's beloved pet, who gives rides to children.

Goat + flying squirrel = who are we kidding, this is a terrible idea. Who authorized this? Now the goats can escape, and they're headbutting things/people/each other at alarming speed.

53

Consider the various approaches to having the power of teleportation with one significant drawback: you can't bring anything with you, even clothes. How might different personality types handle that?

On the one end of the spectrum, you've got the "train in martial arts and become an unstoppable assassin" route.

On the other end, there's the "I just use it to get undressed quickly" approach.

There's also the middle ground where some very curious and dedicated individuals live. The "I've just *got* to see that rare bird up close, even briefly" people. The "I'll skydive without a parachute" crowd. And the "watch me invent a new sport, or perhaps a type of bounty hunting, because I can tackle anything I can see" people.

These, incidentally would be the same to volunteer "Sure I can catch your rare bird; just point it out and get ready with a pillowcase or something. Hope you're not prudish, by the way."

54

Space diplomacy is an interesting job that I'd never want. It's tricky enough on Earth; just imagine the headache that would be trying to arrange an interplanetary banquet.

Start with the regular human variety of foods to avoid for reasons of religion/allergies/etc. Then factor in aliens who eat a whole other type of food; they'd need separate dishes. Okay, do-able.

But then you get some unexpected curveballs. Maybe one species can eat fruit, but not digest it fully, and their cultural doctrine says they must eat it if given the opportunity. Some complicated history about atoning for the extinction of frugivores on their own planet by disseminating the seeds themselves. Now you've got dinner guests with upset stomachs and alien gas.

And then there's another species that considers it blasphemous to eat in front of other people, and whose idea was this dinner party anyway?

55

Here's a worldbuilding idea: cautionary tales for fictional cultures. A lot of classic European fairy tales show wolves as a danger to avoid or outwit — The Three Little Pigs, Little Red Riding Hood, The Boy Who Cried Wolf, etc. What kind of danger might the children in your fictional culture be expected to come up against?

Maybe the mer-babies need to be warned away from boats. A story about The Horrible Things They'll Do To You would cover that.

Maybe centaurs have a nursery rhyme about watching for gopher holes. (It doubles as a counting song, since the kid in the story breaks one leg after another. Optional verses may include healing magics so the song can continue past four.)

Goblin cautionary tales feel more like a game of one-upmanship about who can die the most story-worthy death, but to each their own. Some cultures treat an approaching predator with respect, while others start making bets on who can pull its tail without getting eaten.

56

What would be the most useful electronic item to take into a fantasy world? A smartphone would have some uses, though not many without the satellite network it's made for. A flashlight could be good for certain scenarios. A music-playing device might be fun. A wristwatch would have limited value. What about an electric scooter? Or, while we're at it, an electric car? You could be a proper wizard with that. What else?

And what if, once it's there in that fantasy world, some well-meaning wizard manages to enchant it with "eternal lightning" where the batteries go?

57

Among the most powerful wizards, there's no need to maintain a human shape. I imagine there could be trends and fashions, which would be on display at the annual (centennial?) Wizards' Gala.

Maybe one year they all come as the most colorful animal they can manage — the room is full of peacocks and small dragons with galaxy-print wings.

Maybe another year everyone comes as a tiny creature riding on the shoulder of their most talented apprentice (extra points if the apprentices are illusioned to look like the wizards themselves).

Maybe the year afterward, the trend is to disguise oneself as an inanimate object and trick as many people as possible. Those same apprentices wander around greeting each other politely, and it's anyone's guess which is going to be the first to speak: the hat, the boutonniere, or that single red thread in the bow tie. Extra points if a single person in the ballroom full of fancypants is the type to put googly eyes on something just to throw the others off.

Write about a Wizards' Gala. Whether the wizard you focus on is dignified, spiteful, or an eternal prankster is up to you.

<h1 style="text-align:center">58</h1>

A new challenge for interstellar diplomats: what if a friendly alien race has a different sort of color vision, and either they or the humans have trouble with each other's written communication?

There are plenty of Earth animals that can't see the color red, or can't pick out an orange tiger hiding among green grass. It's not much of a stretch for the aliens to have colors we can't see either. And maybe they like to write with them, the way we prefer black text on a white background.

Just imagine what kind of chaos that colorblindness might cause when it comes to written memos, food packaging, and even pen colors.

(Does someone try to start a business with the "invisible" ink that the other species can't see? It would only work on certain backgrounds, but their customers don't know that.)

59

Consider the gods of animals.

Do you think moths pray to the porch light? Is it a fickle deity, only rewarding the truly devout, or maybe those who solve the riddle of its heat?

Do cats worship the sun, or do they instead consider it an unreliable servant that sometimes falls behind clouds?

Street lights might do double duty in two pantheons: the god of unattainable glory to those moths, and also the god of plentiful meals to the bats that swoop in after them.

60

What kind of musical instruments would different fantasy races favor? I imagine minotaurs and orcs would be fond of drums, and we all know that pixies like pan pipes. What about centaurs? Some sort of stringed instrument, maybe?

Is there a type of music-making thing that we humans haven't thought of yet? Maybe the dragons have something crafted from their shed scales, either clattering together or ringing like tiny gongs or pierced with holes so they whistle when spun through the air. The possibilities are endless. Write about someone nonhuman making music, and their favorite way to do it.

61

Think of a recent inconvenience — at home, at work, in the car — and envision it on a spaceship.

Maybe there's a beeping that no one can find the source of (a wristwatch that fell behind a console).

Maybe the new crewmember's ship cat doesn't get along with the one that's already there, leading to cat fights and passive-aggressive peeing in the cargo hold.

Maybe a piece of electronics isn't working right after getting accidentally/purposefully smacked.

Maybe the space courier wasn't careful with a delivery of rare foodstuffs, and it's leaking through the packaging. The cats will be all over that. Hopefully it doesn't leak onto the electronics.

62

Uses for a magic spell that stops momentum:

* To save someone falling off a building; they'll land safely, if abruptly.

* As the Adrenaline Junkie Adventure Du Jour; jump off buildings on purpose!

* To stop a fight; suddenly swords / fists / beer bottles are just pressed against faces, and nobody is hurt (embarassed though, oh yes).

* In martial arts training; hold nothing back, but hurt no one.

* Pranks. Friend is hammering nails? No he isn't. He's lovingly caressing them with a hammer. Other friend is practicing his golf swing? No he isn't. He's staring into the distance with all the confusion of a golden retriever whose owner only pretended to throw the ball. And when they go after you in irritation, throwing whatever's at hand? You have the answer to that! Too bad a stopped punch can easily turn into noogies, though. You should stand farther away next time.

63

I was thinking about aliens dancing (as you do), and it occurred to me that it would be fun to see a species that does the honeybee communication: they come home from foraging and tell the others where to find food through interpretive dance. The question is how to ramp that up to a civilized species.

Hunter-gatherer level society, with a cool breakdance in the middle of town?

Stock market with a ballet number?

Maybe even spaceships that return to the station with alien astronauts doing a coordinated stomp routine on the outside of the hull in magnetic boots. Sounds like a party to me.

64

What interesting things could come about from envisioning fantasy creatures as newly hatched/born? Griffins learning to fly, dragons shedding for the first time, minotaurs pretending to lock horns that they don't have. Maybe new dryads are carried around like potted plants, and pixies have a larval stage that's the cutest little glowbugs you ever did see.

65

Write about someone with the ability to make the world around them into a musical — everyone breaks into song when they say so. This can be magical, nanotech brain control, or an unexplained superhero power.

Maybe they made a bargain for this power. Maybe they wound up with it on accident. Maybe they know how to use it well, and maybe they don't.

Do they use it for good or evil? It could be awfully handy in robbing a bank: distract everyone with a rousing singalong about money. And on the other hand, it could be equally handy in *stopping* a bank robbery. What would be the most fun to write about?

66

Reimagine everything technological in your life as a magical object.

The cell phone is a scrying crystal.

The lamps are jars of pixie dust, bought fair-trade from the pixies themselves.

The stove is a slab of polished stone, with fire runes for temperature control.

The air conditioner and heater are both the same air elemental, able to blow forth air at any temperature you like. Though it has been known to pretend to be a dragon under the house if any little children ask.

67

I'd love to read a fantasy story about someone who makes food for magical pets. At any technology level, it could be interesting.

Maybe they have to get specially imported flying fruit (fertilized with pixie dust), and prepare it while it's fresh.

Maybe they work in a canned-food factory, and the worker elves are talking about unionizing.

Maybe the fantasy world recently opened a portal to a cyberpunk world, and the person in charge of feeding the unicorns needs to make sure no robot comes in contact with the enchanted alfalfa, *or else*.

68

We've considered making up fantastical creatures by combining real ones, but what about misunderstanding them instead?

They say that a lot of fantasy beasts were inspired by real animals, after all: unicorns could have been rhinos or mutant goats, the cyclops could have been an elephant skull (the nostril hole for the trunk looks like a single eye), and the Questing Beast of Arthurian legend ("head and neck of a snake, the body of a leopard, the haunches of a lion, and the feet of a hart") was a badly-described giraffe.

What kind of thing can we make up on purpose? Maybe a future archaeologist finds a bird skeleton and decides that the wing bones were unadorned stabbing weapons. Maybe some far-ranging traveler gets an idiom wrong, and returns home with the impression that certain rainclouds drop enchanted water that takes the form of cats and dogs. Maybe someone is simply bad at describing things, and tells their friends that peacocks have a hundred eyes.

And depending on what kind of story this is, maybe someone listening goes out to turn their magic or genetic engineering skills toward making a live one. Maybe several.

69

There are so many movies with aliens that can easily disguise themselves to look human. Let's change that up, and put the human character in that position. How do they do it? Are we talking about a Star Trek style alien race, that can be imitated with a bit of makeup? Or does the human need to learn to walk on all fours, or get around on stilts? Are holograms a part of the costume, so the human needs to make sure not to brush up against anyone else?

This works in a fantasy setting too: how long do you think the human will be able to fool the elves with their latex ears? Of course, if it's fantasy, then there may be magic involved. They could blend in with any crowd, at least physically. But no magic can save them from reacting to the food the locals might expect them to eat.

70

I feel like there's a big potential for future-dystopia fiction to include umbrellas as the 24/7 fashion statement. Normal ones, retractable headgear, tiny hover-drones following people about, etc. Anything to cover you from above.

This thought is brought to you by the factoid that spy satellites were good enough several decades ago to take pictures of topless sunbathers. Imagine how good they are now.

71

We've thought about turning modern tech into magic, but what about future tech? I do love a good bit of genre-blending, and sci-fi things can be very fun when put into a fantasy setting. For example:

Cyborgs with limbs of glowing crystals.

Magic wands shaped like blasters, equipped with stun/sleep/kill magic.

A holodeck powered by hallucinogenic mushrooms (and magic).

Food replicators that can recreate anything put into them. Maybe the local wizard is often heard saying "Tea, Earl Grey, hot."

What else can you think of?

72

Vehicles with a life of their own are a well-loved trope, though they don't always explore the full range of possibilities. There are living cars, flying carpets, witches' brooms, and the occasional magical cloud. Plus robot-piloted spaceships, on the sci-fi side of things.

But what other vehicles might be enchanted/enhanced?

Maybe a skateboard that insists on detours to do tricks.

Heelys shoes that get offended if you walk too long without using the wheels.

A magical sled that prefers concrete over snow.

A futuristic fire truck, with AI navigation and hover technology.

An enchanted recliner chair.

A port-a-potty that may or may not be a spaceship with a truly unfortunate choice of cloaking illusions.

What would be worth writing about?

73

I saw a picture of someone with green hair, a lovely shade of leaf-green, and it occurred to me to wonder if there are colors that dryads or plant elementals can color their hair/foliage that would annoy their elders.

(Don't worry about the "how"; this is a world with magic. And if they want to paint over their leaves and deal with a photosynthesis-deficiency, that is their right.)

I'd love to see a goth dryad. Or a little punk-rock flower fairy awkwardly painting the petals on her head, trying to decide where to stick the thorns that she cut from the rosebush. Is tree sap sticky enough to hold them? She'll find out.

74

We've thought about stopping momentum, but what about starting it? Now that's a super power to consider. Touch someone, activate your power, and they feel an impact like Superman hauled off and smacked them.

Press a toe to the street, pause, then a crater implodes below it.

Get your fingertips on a wrecking ball and send it swinging toward your enemy without a word.

Maybe this is a form of super speed, or maybe it's a special thing. Either way, the drama potential is huge when you can rest a hand on something just long enough to lock eyes with the villain.

(And if someone else has the ability to stop moving things suddenly, does that lead to an appropriate nemesis, or a very undignified fight?)

75

Make a list of things that you as a reader would be delighted to find in a book. Things that would make you grab it off the shelf at the bookstore. It can be anything: plot tropes, character types, settings, weird combinations that you can't believe you haven't read about yet.

Found family? Enemies to lovers? Werewolves working as veterinarians? Vampire heists? Short main characters? White-haired elders saving the day? Urban fantasy fae trying to work up a tolerance to iron?

Make a list of as many as possible. Then see what kind of story you can tell with them, using any combination that fits.

Why is the idea of a robot magician so cool? Because it's unexpected? Not supposed to be allowed? A blending of genres, perhaps — high technology belongs on another part of the bookshelf from the part with magic. And if you could do things with magic, why would anyone ever need to invent machinery?

Well, maybe they didn't. Maybe someone from a different planet or dimension did, and then they came to say hello.

And I'll bet those robots would *love* the opportunity to shoot lightning just as much as a meat creature would.

Write about a society that has successfully domesticated bears.

It's a challenge, since there are good reasons why no one's done it in the real world: bears are omnivorous (expensive to feed), slow to mature, resistant to breeding in captivity, not what you'd call docile, and they don't have a herd structure for the humans to lead.

But just imagine if those challenges could be overcome. What would make it necessary? What would make it possible? Maybe the bears in this world are a little different in some regards. Either way it won't be easy. But it will make for Gigantic Teddy Bears That Can Murder Your Enemies, and surely that's worth the difficulty.

78

Which of the electronic devices in your home would be the most benevolent, if it were granted sentience?

Which would be the most dangerous?

This could be in terms of ability or assumed personality. But let's say a Cloud Of Nanites tears through town, or an alien race kicks off their invasion by disrupting our technology, or whatever other justification you prefer. Something causes every device that runs on electricity to suddenly be able to think and act on its own — possibly with new movement abilities or transforming skills if you like.

The question is, how do *your* electronics behave? Is the fridge judgemental and the TV opinionated? What Toy Story scene is happening in the bedroom? Do you own any lightsabers or sonic screwdrivers? And, depending on how you've treated it, what is the first thing that the cell phone in your pocket does?

79

What do you think will be romanticized, centuries in the future? We consider swords to be cool and cloaks elegant, even though we have guns and techno-fleece jackets now. Riding a horse is glamorous; driving a car is mundane. None of those things were special back in the day.

Which of your boring modern things will be The Aesthetic in the future? Will cars be obsolete, replaced by teleporters? Maybe your long boring commute will be sighed over as a quaint pastoral joy by people who go to work by walking through a door.

Maybe your descendants will live on a space station where the only animals are carefully-regulated housepets and livestock. Maybe that bird outside your window, the one that's annoyingly loud and keeps dropping seeds from the birdfeeder everywhere, will be as breathtaking to your great-great-great grandkids as seeing a dragon would be to you.

80

Someone once pointed out to me that if all human-made adhesives suddenly dissolved, the world as we know it would fall apart. That would make for an interesting sort of apocalypse, depending on the range of effect that you decide on for the story.

Maybe it's a magical spell that only covers a small area, or sci-fi nanites that only take out a specific kind of glue. Either way, the possibilities get scarier the longer you think about it. Much of human technology involves adhesives of some sort.

Electronic casings. Electronic interiors — circuit boards are made of fiberglass, and what is fiberglass if not panels of solidified adhesive, around glass threads? So much for fiberglass cars, boats, bathtubs, and water tanks.

And that's not even getting into the dental adhesive, and other medical nightmares.

If all the sticky-stuck things came apart, we'd be reduced to a very dire state indeed.

81

If someone were to ask for a magic spell to reach any part of the ocean from any body of water, there are many interesting ways that could go wrong.

Maybe they were hoping to travel the world for fun, or create a speedy trade business for profit, and didn't think it through.

Maybe they didn't realize that it meant *any* body of water. (Bathtime comes with risks.)

Maybe they didn't realize other things could come through when the magic was active. (Ever get slapped with a kracken tentacle from your drinking glass? It's the kind of experience you won't forget.)

82

Here's something I haven't seen much of: a fantasyland version of seeing-eye-dogs.

This could be a wingless dragon guiding a half-elf into the tavern, with the harness/handle and everything.

Or maybe pixies are known to hire themselves out as bonus eyes, riding on a big person to help out.

Heck, someone could wear an enchanted scarf with eyeball patterns on it, and be able to see things in more directions that the sighted characters can.

83

If you could travel back in time once, on a one-way trip, with the knowledge that you'd be creating an alternate timeline instead of overwriting your own, what would you do? Set yourself up as a wizard far in the past? Bring the good word of gunpowder to a native group before the colonizers arrived? Change recent politics? Prevent a car accident or other personal disaster?

Bear in mind that, if you go to a time when you're alive, there will be two of you. Which could be a pro or a con, honestly.

84

Write about a non-human character treating a human hair the same way a human might treat a feather they find on the ground.

Is this character an animal, an elf, an alien?

Do they react with awe, with germaphobia, with artistic inspiration?

Maybe humans are rare. Maybe their hairs have special qualities. Maybe the hairs need to be disinfected in a three-stage process before the children can play with them. Do the characters follow the established wisdom or not?

85

Underused possibilities for time control:

    * Make plants grow faster (food, flowers, etc)

    * Create authentic-looking "antiques"

    * Keep food from spoiling

    * Repair broken things

    * Chicken eggs: store indefinitely, hatch on demand (if fertilized)

    * Terraform a desert overnight by dumping organic mulch and having it stink for a short time instead of years

    Villain options:

    * Reversible torture

    * Gaslighting ("That tree's always been there; you can't trust your memory.")

    * Reduce any building to its construction materials

    * Threaten to do the same to people

Here's a scenario for you: there is a problem that can only be solved by calling in an expert magician of some kind. Ghosts to banish, a shelf of potions spilled and mixed into a complicated curse, fast-growing magical plants sent by a saboteur; some tricky problem.

The expert spends ten minutes dealing with the problem in absolute secrecy, then emerges victorious and demands an exorbitant fee. What happened in that time?

Did the magician freeze time while they worked, so the problem didn't get worse?

Did the assistant spend the time coaxing the whiny prodigy to fix things, which ended up taking only a moment's thought?

Was the apparent problem just bait to lure the magician through a portal, where time passed differently? Perhaps they did epic battle against a would-be invader.

Or maybe the fix really was that quick, but also that difficult: the fantasy equivalent of "$1 to push a button; $99 to know which button to push."

87

Write about a mistake that turns out well.

Maybe that's a magic spell that doesn't do what it's supposed to. Wrong ingredients, a verbal stumble during the incantation, or the person who provided the spell was a liar. Maybe the results are an unlikely success instead of a disaster.

Or perhaps it's a sci-fi mistake instead: give the robot the wrong programming, stow away on the wrong spaceship, mislabel the vials of nanites in the lab. A lot can come from a mistake — a lot of bad, and a lot of good.

I'm sure you're familiar with the trend of naming fantasy characters in a way that fits their specialty, even if their parents had no way of knowing what they would grow up to do. I've love to see that turned on its head.

"Felix Leon" with the wild blond hair isn't a magical lion, but a frog spirit.

"Alistair de Sanguine" of the pale complexion isn't a vampire, but a pegasus. ("I don't know what you're laughing at; we are a race of noble warriors!")

"Ariel Draconis" with the love of rare steak isn't a dragon, but a plant elemental. (Venus Flytrap. Very few of them about.)

"Delilah Proteanna" of the epic hotness isn't actually a succubus – she's a phoenix, who loves to joke about the hotness thing.

"Hammer" the linebacker is a siren; they come in male form too. His singing voice is amazing.

His buddy "Rocky" may look like a snaggletoothed troll in human form, but he's really a genderqueer unicorn with SUCH a crush on Alistair the pegasus.

89

Imagine you can do some form of color-based magic. Maybe you can summon things from matching colors — bananas from the folds of a yellow raincoat, spare house key from the underside of a car. Maybe touching (or eating) certain colors grants you certain powers — fire control from red things, water control from blue. Maybe you can change other people's moods by touching them with certain colors.

Now imagine that you have been presented with a crisis, and the only colors available are your *least* favorite ones.

90

Everyone talks about time traveling to the past, and worrying about wrecking the future, but there's an intriguing option we're missing: someone could go to the future, do things, then return with no trace of them ever happening. On purpose.

Worried about failing a test, or asking someone out and getting rejected? If you've got a time machine handy, you can skip forward to the big moment and give it a trial run. It feels a little immoral somehow, but the beauty of it is *no one would ever know.*

And then of course there are the villains, who are utterly unconcerned with the morality of the situation. They could get away with all manner of things repeatedly. Who would stop them? Who would even know?

91

Write something heartwarming about a found family.

Maybe it's space pirates reminiscing about childhood holidays, and finding ways to recreate them for each other.

Maybe it's an interaction between house pets, with the stubborn elders finally accepting the newcomer.

Maybe it's college kids estranged from their birth families, or adults who have outlived theirs, or simply close friends who have been there for each other through some very hard times.

There are lots of ways to find a family. And they're all good.

92

A challenge for you: think of a way to hint at magic or super powers that isn't overdone. We've all seen eyes that glow or change color, teeth that grow sharp, ears that get pointy.

I'd love to see a character's eyebrows ripple into tiny scales when they're concentrating on their powers. Or someone's nose disappear when they cast a spell.

What hasn't been done yet?

93

Glow-in-the-dark things look like magic. Imagine introducing them to someone unfamiliar with the concept.

This could be a time travel story — set yourself up as a medieval magician, or a Shakespearean era con artist, or a Mesopotamian god, or simply a witch in the woods whose footpaths are lit by drops of moonlight.

This could also be a space adventure: maybe an alien culture has discovered fire, but not anything that glows without heat. Do they react with awe, suspicion, worship, fear?

This could be a fantasy land jaunt: imagine the reactions of the various magical creatures when you explain that no, it's not magic at all. Just science.

And it doesn't have to have a speculative element at all, if you'd like to write about the moment a toddler sees their first glowstick. Or the child is handed the almighty power of a UV flashlight, and told to light up the stars on their ceiling. The world has never seemed so magical.

94

What happens if a werewolf goes to the moon?

If the sunlight reflecting off the moon's surface is what causes the transformation, then I could see the werewolf getting to choose their form by moving from daytime to nighttime. Kind of the opposite from on Earth: light bounces off the moon during the moon's daytime.

On the other hand, maybe it's not about the light at all; maybe the moon itself is the source of this magic. Maybe a werewolf on the moon turns into something alien and strange, which we've never seen down here on Earth.

95

Characters often return home at the end of the story: after saving the kingdom, or slaying the Dark Lord, or gallivanting about the galaxy. What if they come home in the beginning instead?

Where are they returning from, and what do they find there?

Maybe they just had a classic adventure, or maybe this was just a trip to the big city for a rare book. Maybe they had to travel to the next star system for bioengineering school. Maybe they ran away with a shapeshifter, and are bringing the interspecies kids back to meet the family.

Maybe social drama awaits. Maybe there's a crisis that only their newly-gained knowledge or expertise can solve. Maybe there's a mystery. Maybe a localized apocalypse. Maybe home just *isn't there*, either due to magic, tractor beams, or unknown shenanigans, and it's up to the characters to get it back.

Quick thinking and unorthodox weaponry are always fun. What if the good guys are in a sci-fi tight spot, armed only with futuristic food items to fend off the enemies?

We've seen movies with food pellets that only need a moment in the microwave to become a full meal — piping hot soup, a whole turkey, phosphorescent noodles. Picture those pellets flying through the air, or wedged into strategic locations, with ray guns that can microwave them from a distance.

"Set your phasers on 'baked potato,' and let's do this!"

Moon dust, as it turns out, is an incredible breathing hazard. The particles are tiny and sharp, with no wind and water to round off any pointy bits like on Earth. Prolonged exposure can cause significant lung damage, and all twelve of the astronauts who have walked on the moon reported symptoms afterwards.

One of those twelve had a significant allergic reaction. What are the odds? Surely it's not one in twelve. We have no way of knowing how many humans are allergic to moon dust; we can only speculate.

Being writers, we can also speculate about why.

It could be just random genetic chance, of course, but maybe the moon just likes some people more. Plenty of belief systems have assigned personalities to the moon. Or maybe there are aliens involved, with nanotechnology and their own logic. Possibly an eldritch entity lurking in the void with unknowable priorities and a disturbing range of influence.

And of course there's the werewolf angle, with trace elements of wolf genetics determining whether or not a person can handle moon life, but that hardly needs to be said.

98

Some fantasy races are usually shown as high class (vampires, elves) while others are middle or lower class (werewolves, goblins). Write about a world with that reversed. Any technology level you like.

Perhaps the millionaires take their private helicopters to untouched woodland on the full moon, where they can cover up any unfortunate murders.

Maybe graffiti appears in places that can only be reached by people who can turn into bats.

Maybe the middle-class fashion tends toward makeup with a green tinge, to hint at desirable goblin ancestry.

Maybe the skateboard parks are full of pointy ears and tricks that can only be pulled off by people who are light enough to walk on snow.

99

It seems like the only time we see robots and monsters together is when one is punching the other. There are so many other possibilities. Let's combine some genres! What is the most interesting fantasy creature for a robot to interact with?

Maybe centaurs would appreciate a two-legger fast enough to keep up with them.

Maybe sphinxes just let automatons pass because they've seen that kind of encyclopedic knowledge before, and they might as well save some time.

Maybe all the werewolf families in town hire babysitters with metal skin that the rambunctious cubs can't pierce.

Maybe the servant robot that's slowly learning about humanity is the one to befriend the captured mermaid, or the fairies in the garden.

Or, depending on how badly the humans treat it, the vampire looking for a way in.

"I live on these premises. I welcome you in as an honored guest. It is not against my programming to tell you that I would not be tracked down if I were stolen. My charging cable is in this convenient handbag."

100

What if magic is real and it stays secret because it looks like bad CGI?

People who witness magic in person can always have their minds clouded, as they have been for most of human history, but all this newfangled technology has to be handled a different way. A video camera records exactly what it sees.

So, what it sees is ... something that looks laughably fake. The various secret magicians of the world make a point to keep their spells up to date with the current mundane trends — some of them even have running contests for who can make the most fake-looking spell.

I imagine they have a great time doing it. I sure would.

Don't miss out!

Visit the website below and you can sign up to receive emails whenever Mara Lynn Johnstone publishes a new book. There's no charge and no obligation.

https://books2read.com/r/B-A-FTUT-XGIJC

BOOKS 2 READ

Connecting independent readers to independent writers.

About the Author

Mara Lynn Johnstone grew up in a house on a hill, of which the top floor was built first. She split her time between climbing trees, drawing fantastical things, reading books, and writing her own. Always interested in fiction, she went on to get a Master's Degree in creative writing, and to acquire a husband, son, and three cats. She has published several books and many short stories. She still writes, draws, reads, and enjoys climbing things. She can be found up trees, in bookstores, lost in thought, and on various social media.

Read more at https://www.MaraLynnJohnstone.com.

www.ingramcontent.com/pod-product-compliance
Lightning Source LLC
Chambersburg PA
CBHW022027150726
47990CB00002B/850